POEMS B

Is "With All I

does anoth

Sharon S. Barr

Chrissie Barr Publishing

Poems by Sherri Barr

This book is a collection of poems about children's dreams, love, holidays, the Allegany River and more.

SherriBarrbooks.com

Library of Congress Control Number:
LCCN: 2021911404
Title: Poems by Sherri Barr
Author Name: Sharon S. Barr, 1943

Book Creator: Christie A. Barr

Identifiers:
ISBN-13: 978-1-7373657-5-4 (Paperback)
ISBN- 978-1-7373657-9-2 (Paperback)
ISBN-13: 978-1-7373657-4-7(Hardcover)
ISBN-13: 978-1-7373657-6-1 (eBook/KDP format)
ISBN-13: 978-1-7373657-7-8 (eBook/EPUB format)

Chrissie Barr Publishing

This book is dedicated to my husband Danny
and my family.

It is also dedicated to my English teacher,
Ms. Driscoll, who inspired me to write during
my High School years.

Index

1 A Child's Land
2 Secret Love
3 The Poor Side
4 The Rich Side
5 The Battle
7 Toy Boat
8 Honey – To My Danny
9 To My Mom & Dad
10 Sonnet to a Day
11 Mixed Emotions/Recipe of Life
12 My Guiding Light
13 My Island
14 My Epitaph
15 From Night til Morn
17 My Little Danny Boy
18 Dear Lord
19 Revolution of Life
20 Lost to the Sea
23 Back Home
24 Blizzard of '77
25 Ever Changing
26 Theme of Laziness
27 If Time Would Halt
28 Shady Deal
29 Dating Data
30 The Road
31 An Old-Fashioned Christmas
34 Canning Season
35 With This Ring
36 Leave His Love for Me
37 I'm Not Coming Back
38 Moment You Were Mine
39 I Lost My Baby
40 True Love
41 My River
42 The Poor Man
43 Spring and Winter
44 My Watch Dog Kitty
45 To Terri Lee
46 Love for You
47 Land of Daydreams
48 Pledge of Love
49 To Mark Kenyon
50 Joe & Jan
51 Adventure
52 Johnny Levine
55 Darling I'm Leaving You
56 Happiness of Winter
57 Halloween Trick
59 To My Children
60 Walk Away
61 My Honey
62 Turbulence
63 I Don't Cry
64 Lost Love
65 My Allegheny River

Child's Land

I know I'll never find it
For it is all so good
It's for the little children
Who do the things they should

There are real root beer rivers
And trees are lollipops
There are many gumdrop hills
And ice-cream mountain tops

The grass is made of wintergreen
The homes are gingerbread
There is a goodness all about
And tears are never shed!

The clouds are fluffy frosting
The sky is a lake of blue
Roads are made of chocolate
And there's so many things to do

This is where good children go
When night is on its way
As it eases care from tiny heads
At the end of a wonderful day!

*** Upon Carol Ann Herman's death the director of Children's Mental Institute asked permission to dedicate this to her. She died of pneumonia at age 7.

Secret Love

I often stand in a shadow
Not knowing what to do
Knowing only the heartaches
Of secretly loving you

No one knows who I love
No one knows but me
I try to hide my feelings
And love you secretly

But alas I'm doomed to suffer
For I shall never say
How much I truly love you
A secret that must stay

I know I'll never have you
But I can surely be
The one who loves you truly
Although it's secretly!

The Poor Side

Ah to live in the castle
That overlooks this land
Instead of this lonely cabin
Plowing the earth by hand

I'd be dressed in riches
Diamonds adorning my hair
Men would bow and curtsy
I'd walk in a heavenly air

I'd never have to cook
Or scrub that filthy pan
I could have married wealth
But I took the love of a man

Love isn't everything!
Think what money will buy
It could buy you pleasures
Until the day you die

But alas time cannot be changed
I'd change it if I could
All these are in the past
What's done is done for good

The Rich Side

I married a millionaire
I married a pot of gold
Married a man I didn't love
Whose heart was hard and cold

I love a man in a cabin
A man both simple and poor
A man who asked me to marry
But money I wanted more

My heart has cried a thousand times
A thousand times it bleeds
To go back to his cabin
And to satisfy his needs

Money isn't everything
No love is far more dear
If I could live my life again
It wouldn't be up here

I'd be down in a cabin
Plowing about the land
I'd give up my fortune
To hold this poor man's hand

The Battle

As I look at you in your bed
I see a child carefree
Innocence surrounds your head
How truly happy you must be

To you, my child, war is a game
The good men always win
When you grow up it's not the same
It's burdened then with sin!

I've watched you tote your toy gun
Shoot bad men – face to face
This will be gone, my little son
Lost in times short space!

I've seen you hide behind a tree
As the enemy troops pass by
Then how swiftly you would flee
To give the warning cry!

To Arms, To Arms!! The enemy's near
Take up your guns and fight
Run on, run on and never fear
We'll win for sure tonight

And up in arms your friends would come
Your army, three feet tall!
Their pockets full of sweets and gum
In case in hunger you should fall!

Ah yes – you won your battle
Your foes had met defeat
Your pan hats you would rattle
On toy drums you would beat

Now with your teddy in one arm
Contently there you lie
Not knowing how this childhood charm
Will swiftly pass you by!

If only childhood we could keep
Preserve it through the years
We'd save a lot of restless sleep
And save a thousand tears

But alas the young grow old
And childhood swiftly flies
Age moves in a killer bold
And childhood quickly dies

Toy Boat

Sailing slowly over the pond
Is the raft of a little boy
In his dreams he's on the deck
It's a real ship now, not a toy!

He is the captain in command
Over the wide ocean so blue
Although his men are working hard
They are indeed a stubborn crew

He imagines the ripples on the pond
As waves over ten feet high
His crew is near to mutiny
There is trouble in the sky!

They tie him up and gag him
To throw him to the sea
Then they see a distant speck
It's land!! Oh could this be?

Safe again and in command
He steps upon the shore
He turns his raft the other way
To sail his pond once more!

Honey – To My Danny

Honey, days go by so swiftly
Like the passing of one's dreams
Forty years have gone by
How impossible it seems

Forty years ago
We stood upon the altar
You took my hand in yours
Our words did not falter

As our hearts beat in unison
We vowed our love so true
Our lives became as one
As we both whispered "I do"

The days, the months, the years flew by
Every moment ticked away
Tell me where the time has gone
It seems like yesterday

We've been so busy with our kids
Running them here and there
It sometimes seems impossible
To show each other that we care

But with each passing moment
With every passing day
My love for you has deepened
In every possible way

I would still stand upon the altar
And vow my love so true
For all I ever ask from life
Is to always be with you!

All My Love Forever
Sherri

To Mom & Dad

When I was a little girl
You would take me by the hand
My heart felt the warmth of love
You were parents grand!

As I grew to be a teenager
We clashed in many ways
But the warmth of love was there
Through all those trying days

Now I am a woman
And this I know for sure
The warmth of love is still there
And will through our lives endure

Sonnet to a Day

I saw the golden sun shoot from the sea
I saw its rays set fire to the day
I saw its rays upon the water play
And cast the shadows of each silent tree

A lissome joy within my heart burned free
And as I watch the trees so gently sway
I knelt in silence on the sand to pray
To thank the gracious Lord that I could see!

How long I stayed in that transcendent daze?
How long in silence did I sit and think?
How long upon the soft waves did I gaze?
One whole day! I sat silent on its brink

Until I saw the last of its grand rays
Again into the sea with fury sink!

Mixed Emotions / Recipe of Life

This world is made of love
It's mixed with emotions of hate
It's seasoned with drops of sorrow
Then ground in the bowl of fate

It is blended with grains of grief
And rolled once with great misgiving
It's sifted with grains of pride
And the pain and contempt of the living

It's beaten in the mixer of age
Anger and fear are blended in
It's poured into the pan of passion
And seasoned again with a grin

It's rolled again with joy
Then filled with deep disgust
It's frosted with fond memories
And decorated with trust

It's baked in a warm hearted oven
And placed on the table of a dream
It is cut with the knife of faith
And eaten with tears of cream!

My Guiding Light

I lay asleep at night
And yet I see you still
You're like a guiding light
Upon a steep cold hill

To have you for my own
I must fulfill one deed
To climb the hill alone
To have the one I need!

The hill is dark and steep
There is no hidden lane
Physically the rocks cut deep
Mentally I feel no pain

With each step I take
The mountain grows still more
My arms and legs both ache
My body's lame and sore!

It's impossible to reach you
I cannot climb that hill
For everything I do
The path grows steeper still

To the bottom I sometimes fall
Yet with tears again I try
To you for help I call
But you are deaf to every cry

I dream this dream every night
Each night I wake up crying
For I can't reach my guiding light
And yet I keep on trying!

My Island

There is a little island
In the middle of the sea
A very special island
That's waiting just for me!

To this little island
I am going when I die!
To this little island
In the middle of the sky

I'll shine a thousand halos
I'll mend a million wings
Then I'll grab a fluffy cloud
And listen as an angel sings

When I reach this island
I will save a place for you
And we shall sail across the sky
On a cloud that's built for two!

My Epitaph

Bury me by my rivers side
For this is everything I've known
There in peace I will abide
There in silence we'll travel alone

My epitaph is a simple one
It's easy to understand
I wrote it as the setting sun
Lit up my river grand

"Sunshine, rain, sleet and snow
No matter what the weather'd be
To my river I used to go
And it would comfort me!"

"I knew its every curve and bend
And they in turn knew me
A willing ear it would lend
And my troubles floated free!"

"Here through life I came each day
Here after death I chose to be
Now we're together forever to stay
Forever, my river and me!"

From Night Til Morn

Darling between the night and morn
When the world lies in silent sleep
My heart creeps back to you
With love so true and deep

Our love had been forbidden
But we fought to make them see
How much we loved each other
How together we should be

They knew all the rules of life
Our love was truly wrong
We could not tell them darling
That our love was pure and strong

Though we weren't allowed together
(for they kept us far apart)
We were together in our dreams
Together in our heart

But came a day of sorrow
When we broke up for good
We spoke unkind angry words
From hearts made of wood

My parents liked another boy
His parents liked me too
That's why I married him
Though I was still in love with you!

When he holds my hand
It's you I'm thinking of
When we kiss goodnight
It's you I kiss, my love!

No one knows I love you
My love I'll always hide
I'll give my love to him
By his laws I will abide

How I wish those angry words
Between us were never said
I wish I could tell my parents
The reason for the tears I shed

Now I'll never be happy
For my true love I'll never see
For I have married another boy
And content I must try to be

The hours from sunrise to sunset
Belong only to this boy
I must do my very best
To fill his life with joy

But after he's asleep
Those hours are mine alone
To cherish fond memories of you
And the love I'll never own.

My Little Danny Boy (3 years old)

I know a little boy
As sweet as he can be
He is a little rugger
And means the world to me

He is cute and cuddly
But he has an impish air
From the tips of his little toes
To the tousles in his hair

When he says his prayers at night
And I tuck him into bed
He looks just like an angel
I regret the things I said

He makes my whole life happier
He fills it full of joy
I am so very proud of him –
He is my "little" Danny boy!!

Dear Lord

Dear Lord, how I hate to write
Please hear my prayers tonight
In this land of the free
There is so much tyranny
I ask you this how can it be?

Dear Lord, the taxes that I pay
They soar higher day by day
In this land of the free
I don't know how this can be
I just ask you this help me to see!

Dear Lord, look at the mess they've made
Good God I find I'm overpaid!
If I could have earned less
Life would not be such a mess
I'd be entitled to food stamps and Medicaid!

Dear Lord, oh how I hate to write
Please see our helpless plight
In this land we love so much
They use goodness for a crutch
I ask you this give it your touch!

Dear Lord, please look down and see
Just what they're doing to me
In this land of the free
If they'd leave my paycheck be
I know I could take better care of me!!

Revolution of Life

Ah, Rise the sun in youthful beauty rare
Awakening each carefree newborn day
As noon comes nigh it's creased with care
And it has lost its youthful carefree ray

Then sinks the sun in fury burdened fire
Resigning to its peace and rich domain
The sun which once had seemed to never tire
Now sinks to the ground in a burst of pain

Rise up, bold moon, look o'er the day gone by
Look not upon the sorrows in the past
Think not of sadness as you pace the sky
Upon the future rays of silver cast

Yes, life is like the revolutions of the earth
So with one's death begins another birth

Lost to the Sea

Far away on an island
Far away out to sea
On this paradise island
My husband waits for me

He walks on billowy cushions
Restless all the while
Yet I know that he is happy
I can see his gentle smile

Ah yes he was a good man
Known throughout the town
But he was always restless
And couldn't settle down

His grandfather was a sailor
His father a captain true
He always seemed so restless
He loved the ocean too!

After we were married
We moved to an island small
He seemed to settle down
Ignore the restless call

But day by day I noticed
He would softly sigh
He lost his gentle smile
And the twinkle in his eye

One day at dawn I woke
I felt a sudden chill
His bed lay there untouched
The hut was oh so still

I walked all around it
Then down to the water's edge
There he stood by the ocean
Uttering a solemn pledge

He said he had to leave me
For just a little while!
I noticed the twinkle in his eyes
And the happiness in his smile

"Just once more" he pleaded
"Oh Darling let me go,
This yearning that's inside me
Will be my death I know!"

"Oh Darling I am dying,
I'm longing for the sea
I was born a sailor
And never will be free!"

"I promise I'll be back
Just let me sail once more,
I've got to find the answer,
The thing I'm searching for."

Then I let him go
I knew from the very start
I'd never really have him
For the sea had won his heart!

Each night I prayed for him
To return safely home to me
I prayed he'd end his search
And leave that dreadful sea

Not long after he had gone
I gave birth to his son
I prayed to the mighty Lord
To spare my little one

We moved away from the ocean
I gave him all I had
I never mentioned the ocean
Or told him of his dad!

One day he came to me
"Mother – what is wrong?
No matter what I do
My days are oh so long!"

I saw his father's spirit
Growing swiftly in his soul
His father died at sea
And this would be his goal

As if destiny had called him
And beckoned him away
Told him of his father's fate
And taunted him to stray

My son now knew the reason
Why he loved the sea
He asked for my forgiveness
And left to face his destiny

When he went aboard the ship
He sadly threw me a kiss
"I'll return to you dear mother
I solemnly promise this!"

I knew as his ship set sail
He'd be happy for awhile
For there upon his lips I saw
His father's gentle smile

I knew as his ship set sail
I'd lost him to the sea
For he was born his father's son
And never would be free

Back Home

The trees back home are dressed
In their soft white fleecy gowns
The ground is covered white
In all the surrounding towns

The hills that surround our city
Like a crown that surrounds a head
Are full of happy people
Trodding along with their sled

The Christmas Lane is lit
And arches across the street
It's decorated with snow
It's trimmed with lights so sweet

Uptown there are people shopping
Trodding happily through the snow
There is Christmas spirit everywhere
And cheeks are all aglow

There is ice upon our skating pond
The bon fires blazing bright
People are singing merrily
As they glide into the night

Upon the hills they're skiing
Toboggans glide to and fro
A sight that'll warm the coldest heart
And will make the spirit glow

Where I am right now
The sun is warm and high
Flowers are all in bloom
Palm trees reach the sky

People are dressed in shorts
Christmas spirit is few
How I wish I were back home
In the snow I love so true!!

Blizzard of '77

Through my window I saw it
A mountainous wall of white
Sweeping down the hillside
Hiding the slope from sight

Driven by the shrieking winds
A blizzard of hellish force
Battering everything in its way
Along its ferocious course

The children were at school
I felt the chill of fear
I must go after them
They'd never make it here

I donned my warmest clothing
I knew which way they'd come
Through the knee deep snow I trod
The wind had lessened some!

I saw them bobbing through the snow
I called but they couldn't hear!
The driving snow was blinding
My vision wasn't clear

Should they fall into a snowdrift
They'd suffocate for sure
My weary legs went faster
I prayed, God, I could endure

I swept them into my arms
Then I held them by the hand
I led them safely home
Through that winter wonderland

How good to step inside that door
And feel the warmth that's there
Secure within my cozy home
From the force of the wintry air

Ever Changing

The rose has lost its beauty
The tree has shed its gown
The river is frozen over
The snow falls silently down

The softness of the white clouds
Suddenly has turned to grey
The animals have gone to bed
The birds have flown away

The breeze has grown colder
The bees no longer buzz
Now all that's left is memories
Of life as it once was

Theme of Laziness

They lay beneath their covers
That dreary winter day
He said "get up and start the fire"
She said "I'm going to stay!"

"Get up and work the bellows
Just make a little breeze!"
And up she spoke a shiverin'
"I think I'd rather freeze!"

"Get up!" spoke he in an angry tone
"Get up and do thy chores!"
She answered back annoyingly
"They're not my chores – but yours!"

He said "get up you lazy thing"
She simply answered "No!"
Colder it got – still colder
But neither would relent and go!

Now they lay beneath the soil
Both of them are dead
Because they both were lazy
And wouldn't get out of bed!

If Time Would Halt

If only time would halt awhile
And we could go carefree
Back to the days of childhood
And the way it used to be

When our cheeks were pretty rosebuds
And our hands were soft and white
When our hearts were full of love
As we said our prayers at night

When our lives were full of laughter
And our hearts were full of fun
When our dreams were always peaceful
And we slept with the setting sun

But alas time will not halt
And these things are of the past
I'll lock them into my memory vault
As time moves on so fast

Shady Deal

I walked through the door and was sitting at the bar
When a Texan drove up in his shiny new car
He sat on a stool right next to me
And by the smell of his breath – he was drunk as could be

He bragged and bragged about all of his dough
And ideas in my head soon started to grow
I told him I was a better gambler then he
And he bet his car that I couldn't be!

I pulled out a coin and gave it a toss
The poor little Texan suffered the loss
I jumped in his car and gave a big squeal
I had beaten the Texan and won the deal

There is a moral to this little rhyme
Watch out for the stranger with his two headed dime!!!

Dating Data

A biology student never date
He cuts up everyone
Never date a baseball player
He likes to hit and run

Always shun a track star
For he is always fast
Beware of the football heroes
They've made passes in the past

But marry a tennis player
For him open all doors
He has a wonderful racquet
But in love he always scores!!

The Road

Wandering, winding, turning it goes
Like a big brown lake roughly it flows
At often times this road is rough
And traveling forward may seem tough

But if you lift your chin and hum a tune
The road again will be smooth soon
Always forward, forward run
Don't turn back for anyone

When you're in a rut get up and go
Or more hardships you will know
Get up, move on, though it's a mess
These are but trials on the road to success

An Old-Fashioned Christmas

Gather round Children
While I tell with delight
A story about Christmas
In an old-fashioned light

The trees would be laden
And heavy with snow
Drifting and swirling
As the cold winds blow

It was on such a day
That my father and me
Would trudge through the woods
For the best Christmas tree

Though the cold wind roared
And snow bit our face
We'd search on merrily
At a hearty pace

Ah, picture that children
How my father and me
Would sing as we searched
For a tall Christmas tree

Then when we found one
We liked best of all
We'd chop with our axes
Until it would fall

Then we'd tie on our ropes
And away we would go
Tugging it happily
On through the snow

When we reached home
There were shouts of glee
And we sat before the fire
And told about our tree

While we were gone
The women would bake
Every type of cookie
They knew how to make

There were Santas and angels
And wreaths and rings
Sleighs and canes
And so many things

The girls had made popcorn
Which we strung on the tree
It was the grandest sight
My eyes could see

Then we'd stand back
For a moment to admire
The finest Christmas tree
Anyone could desire

After we trimmed it
With a glow on our face
We'd sit and tell stories
By the warm fire place

All of us gathered
At my mother's knee
While we sang Christmas Carols
And the house rang with glee

Then we'd hang up our stockings
And crawl into bed
And we'd dream through the night
Of Santa and his sled

In the morn we'd awaken
(At the first crack of dawn)
We'd ask mom and dad
To see if Santa was gone

There'd be dresses and shirts
Mrs. Claus had made
And toys that the elves carved
With their tiny knife blade

We'd take down our stockings
And find a rare treat
Candies and apples
And good things to eat

As mom cooked the turkey
The aroma filled the air
And our Kinfolk would gather
Our fine feast to share

Each brought a dish
The food filled our table
We ate and we ate
Until we just weren't able

After visiting all evening
We'd say good bye to all
This was the finest Christmas
I could ever recall

This was our type of Christmas
When I was so small!!

Canning Season

It's canning season
Can't you smell?
The pure sweet aroma
Of mom's homemade jel!

The sweet tasty aroma
From mom's jelly bag
That hangs from the line
With a hands off tag

Isn't it wonderful?
The spicy smell
Of the cooking pickles
We know so well

We've washed jars and lids
We've sliced and peeled
We've packed them in juice
Now they are sealed

Then into the canner
To cook until done
Then onto the table
Isn't this fun!

We all sit and listen
For the snap of the lids
With echoes of delight
From each of the kids

We have them all lined
On the shelves so neat
But now we've discovered
They are to pretty to eat!

With This Ring

You gave me a gumball ring
When we were only three
You said you'd be my husband
You vowed to marry me

In your wagon you'd pull me
Or ride me on your bike
We were always very close
And so very much alike

Remember when we were nine
You gave me my first kiss
You told me that you loved me
That I'd be your little miss

When we reached sweet sixteen
I wore your high school ring
You foretold our future
And the happiness it would bring

Now that we are twenty-one
These loving words you said
I love you so much darling
With these rings we'll wed

Our vows we both fulfilled
And together here we stand
Happily facing the future
Together, hand in hand!

Leave His Love for Me

Take away the mountains
Or take away the sea
Take the beautiful rainbow
But leave his love for me

Take away the sun
Take the stars away
Take away all my friends
Or turn the blue skies grey

Take away the flowers
Or cover up the moon
Take away the pretty birds
That hum so sweet a tune

Take away the green grass
Take my lovely willow tree
Take away my life
But leave his love for me

Take away the white clouds
That sail about the sky
But if you take his love
I will surely die!

Leave him here for me
Forever here to stay
Take away everything else
But not his love I pray!

I'm Not Coming Back

You've always had your own way
No matter what we'd do
We broke up at your command
You said that we were through!

You said you loved another
That your love was mine no more
As I shed unhappy tears
You walked out the door

My broken heart has mended
I've found a love so true
Now you say you love me
And want me back with you

But I'm not coming back
You'll break my heart no more
For I have found a truer love
Since you walked out the door

And yet darling I love you
My love is yours alone
Although I am a fool
My love you'll always own

How truly spoiled you have been
All girls belong to you
We were all at your command
You told us what to do

But that's all in the past
I know I was your fool
I'll chalk it up to knowledge learned
As I went through life's school.

Moment You Were Mine

The moment you were mine
I held you close to me
Now you've gone and left me
And I don't care to be

In your eyes that look of love
I thought was cupids sign
Oh how I cherish in my heart
The moment you were mine

My heart cried out a million times
My darling – I love you
As I kissed your tender lips
You said you loved me too

Now you've left me hanging
Like a puppet on a line
And all I have are memories
Of the moment you were mine

Darling I still love you
Even though you hurt me so
I'd take you back again
Why? I'll never know!

I Lost My Baby

I lost my baby one stormy night
I waved and smiled as she drove from sight
What lay in the shadows I could not see
But I knew she'd never come back to me

The thunder and lightning clashed that night
But my baby drove on like a bird in flight
That night I lost my guiding star
For she drove head on into another car

I heard the crash from where I stood
And I knew my baby was gone for good
My baby's gone – she's mine no more
But she's waiting for me at the golden door

Nothing can calm the tears I shed
Nor bring back my baby, from the valley of the dead

True Love

There is in all the world
Nothing like true love
True love finer than rich silk
True love purer than a dove

True love can move a mountain
Or fill an empty sea
It can make one sorrowful
Or fill a heart with glee

Nothing in all this world
Is finer then true love
For it comes from the purest heart
And is guided from above!

My River

See my beautiful river
Wandering to and fro
Watch the water ripple
See it moving slow

Look upon its peacefulness
See how quietly it goes
Like the whispering of a secret
Silently it flows

To see my peaceful river
And to know it's always there
Makes all my troubles vanish
Into its fish scented air

How much I love this river
You shall never know
Here I soothe my heartaches
Here I always go

I salute you, my river
My everlasting friend
For you will always be here
A helping hand to lend

The Poor Man

The heart of a poor man is filled with grief
He is treated no better than a robber or thief
Sorrow and hardships are all that he's known
No land is his – no home of his own

But he'll give up his soup to a hungry child
When his stomach is empty and going wild
He is first to lend a helping hand
Wherever, whenever it is in demand

Happy he sleeps on his lumpy bed
Hunger he's known or for supper some bread
Yet he is the one who is taxed so high
A poor man he'll live – a poor man he'll die!

Spring and Winter

When winter is over
How happy I will be
Just think of all the pretty sights
That now you cannot see

The sky is dark and cloudy
The wind blows through your hair
Snow comes pelting all about
Winter is everywhere!

Someday spring will come again
The sun will shine so bright
Then all that's wrong with winter
Will once again be right

Flowers blooming everywhere
Trees are dressed in green
Rivers flow so freely
Happy sights are seen

It is all so depressing
To see life now so blue
As winter comes a calling
And you don't know what to do

But memories of happy spring
That seems so far away
Makes the future brighter
And brightens up the day

My Watch Dog Kitty

I once had a little black kitty
The stripe on his back was so pretty
I'd walk downtown with him under my arm
And people would vanish as if by some charm

When my kitty manufactures his own perfume
It smells up the house so I air out each room
One day a prowler snuck into my room
My cat gave a hiss and let out his perfume

The prowler ran as fast as he could
From that day on – he vowed to be good
One day my kitty got caught in a tree
I called the firemen to set him free

They climbed up the ladders and got a good look
Their bodies trembled and their ladders shook
Nice kitty! Pretty kitty! Was all they could say
I noticed they buried their clothes that same day

Another day when chased by a dog
My kitty stood upon an old rotten log
The dog came closer – closer he came
Kitty lifted his tail and the dog was aflame

He streaked through the gate, away he did go!
What became of him then I'll never know
Never! Not Once! Have I ever stunk
Like the people squirted by my little skunk

I love my skunk – I think he's so pretty
And I'm very proud of my watch dog kitty

To Terri Lee

As I look into your cradle
And I see you lying there
I think how wonderful you are
Lying there without a care

When the angels bend so low
As to kiss you on the cheek
You smile the cutest smile
And from one sleepy eye you peek

Ah, you chubby cheeked cherub
You're a precious little tot
How much your mommy loves you
How much faith in you she's got

You dimpled little darling
Sweet angel that you are
You little pink bundle from heaven
You're bright as the evening star

How good God has been to us
To send you from above!
To grow to be a woman
As living proof of our love

Love for You

You can follow the endless rainbow
To count each piece of Gold
Count each drop of rain that falls
In the mighty sea I'm told

You can count every blade of grass
And every flake of snow
And every grain of the desert's sand
And every star aglow

Count all the leaves upon the trees
Count every drop of dew
But you could never measure
My endless love for you

Land of Daydreams

I often sit and daydream
Of lands so far away
Lands I know I'll never see
I see most everyday

Many times my mind does go
To some things in my past
Things I have remembered
Memories that forever last

In my land of daydreams
The futures always bright
I see myself as happy as
A never dimming light

Sometimes I dream selfishly
Of things I'd like to see
And things that I am not
I want most of all to be

But the dreams I like to have
I know shall never end
Are dreams of being happy
In the presence of a friend

I can do most anything
Just from where I stand
This is my own private world
My own very precious land

Pledge of Love

My Pledge of love Darling
I give to only you
For I will love you always
With a love so true

I'll always love you Darling
In sickness or in health
And I will go on loving you
In poverty or wealth

I shall date no others
For it's you that I adore
And I would sooner die
Then to love another more

I shall kiss no other lips
Nor hold another's hand
For my Darling I love you
And by your side I'll stand

This is my Pledge of Love
Now I am bound to stay
In your arms forever
Yes – forever and a day

To Mark Kenyon

We have a special neighbor
Who brightens up each day,
He is always kind and thoughtful
And caring in every way.

He's very good to our children
Carting them everywhere
He piles them into his car
Even their friends – he doesn't care,

He takes them bowling on Saturdays
He buys cokes when they pick up a split!
He keeps their scores for them
And he doesn't mind a bit.

He's always there to lend a hand
Or an ear if the case should be,
That's why we think so much of him
And enjoy his company.

He has a witty way about him,
And if he should see a frown,
He turns it into a smile,
He never lets us down!

We are always glad to see him,
And now you can see why
On this special day we say –
"Merry Christmas to a wonderful guy!"

To Joe & Jan

I know this is a little late
But better late than never
To say how much we care for you
And hope our friendship lasts forever

We've helped each other in the past
And we have come to be
Not just friends and neighbors
No! More like Family!!

We have a lot of memories
Of all the things we've done
For our families have been close
And we've had a lot of fun

Even when problems rise
And our tempers even flare
We talk them out together
That's what makes our friendship rare

And through it all its strengthened
Like leather ties that bind
Better friends and neighbors
I know we'll never find!

Adventure

To look at the water and ponder there
And breathe the trout filled river air
And see the fisherman on the lake
Makes the heart of a sailor break

Sure, he knew adventures on the sea before
And traveled to many an unfriendly shore
Brave he was in the days of old
Happy memories he does hold

Gone are the days of the untamed sea
Gone are the pirates who wandered free
Now there are motorboats churning away
All thoughts of adventure – gone astray!

Yet to the sailor who looks from the shore
The adventures still there forever more

Johnny Levine

Years ago there lived a lad
A small boy, three-foot three
He carried a toy gun in his hand
And a toy drum on his knee

Johnny had a brother David
A lad of thirteen years
Johnny saw his brother die
Amidst the British jeers

They said he was a traitor
A traitor to the King
Because Johnny was only eight
He couldn't do a thing

His father a British Soldier
Watched his own son die
He turned away with deaf ears
Ignored his son's last cry

Johnny ran to his father
As tears ran down his face
He swore to avenge David's death
Or forever live in disgrace

Why didn't his father stop them?
Why did he let David die?
David hated his father
Now Johnny knew why

Ten years had passed since then
Johnny grew tall and strong
He ran away from home
To right his father's wrong

It was the year of seventeen seventy
When Johnny went off to war
He never spoke to his father
But kissed his mother at the door

Each time he shot a red coat
He'd sadly notch his gun
Although he hated killing
He would fight till the job was done

One day he heard the bushes move
He carefully pulled them apart
For the sight that lay before him
Pierced like an arrow to his heart

His father lay there wounded
With pleas of mercy in his eyes!
Johnny's heart was full of hate
A hatred that never dies

Johnny's gun went to his shoulder
Slowly he took his aim
But just for a moment he paused
He felt a twinge of shame

He counted the notches on his gun
In all they numbered thirteen
One for each year David lived
Exactly the age of David Levine

He couldn't kill his father
He turned to walk away
He tripped, the gun went off
His father was hit by the ricochet

He ran swiftly to his father
And before his father died
He begged his son's forgiveness
And to be buried at David's side

He carried his father home
And buried him beneath the tree
He laid him at his brother's side
So in peace the two would be

Darling I'm Leaving You

Darling I'm leaving you
Going away with another
In my heart I am lonesome
For you, my love, and no other

You know why I must leave
So you can again be free!
You're in love with another woman
You're no longer in love with me

I'll not make you unhappy
I'll let you wander free
I'll not torture you honey
By making you stay with me!

Though I'm leaving you darling
My heart is heavy and worn
On my back you've placed a cross
And in my heart a thorn

Please come back, my Darling
Please come back and stay
I'll bear my cross of sorrow
And wait patiently for that day

Darling I'm leaving you
Going away with another
But in my heart I'm lonesome
For you, my love, and no other

Happiness of Winter

Snow is swirling in feathery lace
Frosty pictures are every place
Trees are dressed in a fleecy gown
And more snow comes swirling down

Little kids have rosy noses
Snowmen hold their gallant poses
Rivers are stopped by glassy ice
Fireplaces are warm and nice

Children sliding down the hill
Laughing gaily at the thrill
Skaters gliding on the pond
Frozen over by a magic wand

Children playing in the snow
Happy faces all aglow!
This is winter cold and good
People laughing like they should!

Halloween Trick

The moon lay beyond the ridge
Its moonbeams streaked across the bridge
A weird breeze was in the air
Willow trees bowed everywhere

Beyond the bridge there was a farm
Surrounded by an eerie charm
The window shutters bang and creak
Late at night weird things shriek

I swear I saw a witch I do!
Dressed in black, stirring a brew
It's funny how it all begun
The house was still in the noonday sun

I entered the house through a broken door
And walked across the dust filled floor
Oh Lord, the door locked shut outside
All my spirits swiftly died

I couldn't escape it was plain to see
Whatever it was – was after me!
I screamed and screamed – but no reply
I sat and watched the moon rise high

I huddled in the corner of the little room
Then I saw something on a flying broom
I was scared – needless to say
I knelt on my knees to pray

A shrieking laughter filled my ears
My eyes filled with frightened tears
Would I live – again to be seen
Then I remembered it was Halloween!

Witches and goblins are out to scare
Then I heard a moan somewhere
Then I saw her standing there
An ugly old witch with scraggly hair

Bong, bong, the clock struck midnight
My stomach felt like birds in flight
You'll never guess what happened then
And I swear I'll never go there again!

Something grabbed me from the back
All at once the room went black!
When I came to there they stood
My friends laughing as hard as they could

When they told me it made me sick
For all this nightmare was a Halloween Trick!

To My Children

What better time to tell you
How much you mean to me
Five nicer children in this world
No one will ever see

I've been sitting here thinking
Of the things I'd like to say
My heart is bursting with pride
For today is Mother's Day

Five beaming faces
Trying so hard to be
On their best behavior
They mean so much to me

Walk Away

Walk away while you still can
Run away from my jealousy
I will hurt you with distrust
With me you'll never be free

I want to hold you in my arms
Run my fingers through your hair
Hold your body close to me
And tell you that I care

Walk away while you still can
Before I lock you in my cage
Before you become my possession
Before my passion turns to rage

Walk away while you still can
Don't turn back to look at me
All I can do is hurt you now
Our love was never meant to be

As the rain comes pouring down
So do tears within my heart
Walk away while you still can
A new life, my darling, start!!

My Honey

He's my everyday companion
On him I can depend
Forty-nine years of marriage
My Love to him I send

He is a father to five
A grandfather to ten
Great grandpa to two
A wonderful man amongst men!

I'll Love You Forever

Turbulence

The turbulent storm sky thickens
With a depth beyond despair
Filled with bottled rage
That could lash out anywhere

The black clouds heave and grumble
As rain tears fall swiftly down
Winds rape the helpless land
As lightening crashes to the ground

The wrath that was unleashed
Slowly turns the other way
Its sobs then turn to sighs
As it gives in to a brighter day

I Don’t Cry

I don’t cry – my eyes weep
Straight faced composure I keep
Gone are those days when I cried
Gone forever locked inside

Tears flow from deep within
To cry, to weep, would be a sin
In time a broken heart will mend
Emotions ever silent will not end!

Somewhere out there – someone cares
These very feelings someone shares

Lost Love

Grey skies with depth beyond imagination
Relentless raindrops splashing to the ground
A dazed deer dashing through the woods
Barren land laying all around

Hope sparks than dwindles like a flame
Endless days merge into night
A rapid heartbeat racing onward
All surrendering to its plight

Winds weeping through the willow trees
Rustling autumn leaves before they die
The howling hound hearing trouble amidst
Depth and despair of the mourner's cry

The raging river swollen and confined
The tragic thunderbolt crashing from above
The murky maze made by the fog
Could not, would not, match lost love!

My Allegheny River

Did you ever stop to look
About the world so large
And see the trees and rivers
The water and a barge?

The trees in serene silence
The rivers flowing slow
And often when I'm troubled
It's here I like to go

I sit amid the peacefulness
All care is from my head
I sit and think – yes to think
And not a word is said

To sit and watch the water
Ripple slowly past
Is like a happy moment
That should forever last

I saw the shadows on it
A fish jumps here and there
And all I do is sit and think
And breathe the river air

My beloved Allegheny
Is where I'll always be
Sitting on my beloved banks
Happy and carefree

CPSIA information can be obtained
at www.ICGtesting.com
Printed in the USA
JSHW020809240821
17905JS00001BA/35

9 781737 365747